Oh! Well! You Know How Women Are! and Isn't That Just Like a Man

(Irvin Shrewsbury Cobb and Mary Roberts Rinehart)

She emerges from the shop. She is any woman, and the shop from which she emerges is any shop in any town. She has been shopping. This does not imply that she has been buying anything or that she has contemplated buying anything, but merely that she has been shopping--a very different pursuit from buying. Buying implies business for the shop; shopping merely implies business for the clerks.

As stated, she emerges. In the doorway she runs into a woman of her acquaintance. If she likes the other woman she is cordial. But if she does not like her she is very, very cordial. A woman's aversion for another woman moving in the same social stratum in which she herself moves may readily be appraised. Invariably it is in inverse ratio to the apparent affection she displays upon encountering the object of her disfavor. Why should this be? I cannot answer. It is not given for us to know.

Very well, then, she meets the other woman at the door. They stop for conversation. Two men meeting under the same condition would mechanically draw away a few paces, out of the route of persons passing in or out of the shop. No particular play of the mental processes would actuate them in so doing; an instinctive impulse, operating mechanically and subconsciously, would impel them to remove themselves from the main path of foot travel. But this woman and her acquaintance take root right there. Persons dodge round them and glare at them. Other persons bump into them, and are glared at by the two traffic blockers. Where they stand they make a knot of confusion.

But does it occur to either of them to suggest that they might step aside, five feet or ten, and save themselves, and the pedestrian classes generally, a deal of delay and considerable annoyance? It does not. It never will. If the meeting took place in a narrow passageway or on a populous staircase or at the edge of the orbit of a set of swinging doors or on a fire escape landing upon the front of a burning building, while one was going up to aid in the rescue and the other was coming down to be saved--if it took place just outside the Pearly Gates on the Last Day when the quick and the dead, called up for judgment, were streaming in through the portals--still would they behave thus. Where they met would be where they stopped to talk, regardless of the consequences to themselves, regardless of impediment to the movements of their fellow beings.

Having had her say with her dear friend or her dear enemy, as the case may be, our heroine proceeds to the corner and hails a passing street car. Because her heels are so high and her skirts are so snug, she takes about twice the time to climb aboard that a biped in trousers would take. Into the car she comes, teetering and swaying. The car is no more than comfortably filled. True, all the seats at the back where she has entered are occupied; but up at the front there still is room for another sittee or two. Does she look about her to ascertain whether there is any space left? I need not pause for reply. I know it already, and so do you. Midway of the aisle-length she stops and reaches for a strap. She makes an appealing picture, compounded of blindness, helplessness, and discomfort. She has clinging vine written all over her. She craves to cling, but there is no trellis. So she swings from her strap.

The passengers nearest her are all men. She stares at them, accusingly. One of them bends forward to touch her and tell her that there is room for her up forward; but now there aren't any seats left. Male passengers, swinging aboard behind her, have already scrouged on by her and taken the vacant places.

In the mind of one of the men in her immediate vicinity chivalry triumphs over impatience. He gives a shrug of petulance, arises and begs her to have his seat. She is not entitled to it on any ground, save compassion upon his part. By refusing to use the eyes in her head she has forfeited all right to special consideration. But he surrenders his place to her and she takes it.

The car bumps along. The conductor, making his rounds, reaches her. She knows he is coming; at least she should know it. A visit from the conductor has been a feature of every one of the thousands of street-car rides that she has taken in her life. She might have been getting her fare ready for him. There are a dozen handy spots where she might have had a receptacle built for carrying small change--in a pocket in her skirt, in a fob at her belt, in her sleeve or under her cuff. Counting fob pockets and change pockets, a man has from nine to fifteen pockets in his everyday garments. If also he is wearing an overcoat, add at least three more pockets to the total. It would seem that she might have had at least one dependable pocket. But she has none.

The conductor stops, facing her, and meanwhile wearing on his face that air of pained resignation which is common to the faces of conductors on transportation lines that are heavily patronized by women travelers. In mute demand he extends toward her a soiled palm. With hands encased in oversight gloves she fumbles at the catch of a hand bag. Having wrested the hand bag open, she paws about among its myriad and mysterious contents. A card of buttons, a sheaf of samples, a handkerchief, a powder puff for inducing low visibility of the human nose, a small parcel of something, a nail file, and other minor articles are disclosed before she disinters her purse from the bottom of her hand bag. Another struggle with the clasp of the purse ensues; finally, one by one, five coppers are fished up out of the depths and presented to the conductor. The lady has made a difficult, complicated rite of what might have been a simple and a swift formality.

The car proceeds upon its course. She sits in her seat, wearing that look of comfortable self-absorption which a woman invariably wears when she is among strangers, and when she feels herself to be well dressed and making a satisfactory public appearance. She comes out of her trance with a start on discovering that the car has passed her corner or is about to pass it. All flurried, she arises and signals the conductor that she is alighting here. From her air and her expression, we may gather that, mentally, she holds him responsible for the fact that she has been carried on beyond her proper destination.

The car having stopped, she makes her way to the rear platform and gets off-- gets off the wrong way. That is to say, she gets off with face toward the rear. Thus is achieved a twofold result: She blocks the way of anyone who may be desirous of getting aboard the car as she gets off of it, and if the car should start up suddenly, before her feet have touched the earth, or before her grip on the hand rail has been relaxed, she will be flung violently down upon the back of her head.

From the time he is a small boy until he is in his dotage, a man swings off a car, facing in the direction in which the car is headed. Then, a premature turn of a wheel pitches him forward with a good chance to alight upon his feet, whereas the same thing happening when he was facing in the opposite direction would cause him to tumble over backward, with excellent prospects of cracking his skull. But in obedience to an immutable but inexplicable vagary of sex, a woman follows the patently wrong, the obviously dangerous, the plainly awkward system.

As the conductor rings the starting bell, he glances toward a man who is riding on the rear platform.

"Kin you beat 'um?" says the conductor. "I ast you--kin you beat 'um?"

The man to whom he has put the question is a married man. Being in this state of marriage he appreciates that the longer you live with them the less able are you to fathom the workings of their minds with regard to many of the simpler things of life. Speaking, therefore, from the heights of his superior understanding, he says in reply:

"Oh, well, you know how women are!"

We know how women are. But nobody knows why they are as they are.

Please let me make myself clear on one point: As an institution, and as individuals, I am for women. They constitute, and deservedly too, the most popular sex we have. Since away back yonder I have been in favor of granting them suffrage. For years I have felt it as a profound conviction that the franchise should be expanded at one end and abridged at the other--made larger to admit some of the women, made smaller to bar out some of the men. I couldn't think of very many reasons why the average woman should want to mix in politics, but if she did wish so to mix and mingle, I couldn't think of a single valid reason why she should not have full permission, not as a privilege, not as a boon, but as a common right. Nor could I bring myself to share, in any degree, the apprehension of some of the anti-suffragists who held that giving women votes would take many of them entirely out of the state of motherhood. I cannot believe that all the children of the future are going to be born on the first Tuesday after the first Monday in November. Surely some of them will be born on other dates. Indeed the only valid argument against woman suffrage that I could think of was the conduct of some of the women who have been for it.

To myself I often said:

"Certainly I favor giving them the vote. Seeing what a mess the members of my own sex so often make of the job of trying to run the country, I don't anticipate that the Republic will go upon the shoals immediately after women begin voting and campaigning and running for office. At the helm of the ship of state we've put some pretty sad steersman from time to time. Better the hand that rocks the cradle than the hand that rocks the boat. We men have let slip nearly all of the personal liberties for which our fathers fought and bled--that is to say, fought the Britishers and bled the Injuns. Ever since the Civil War we have been so dummed busy telling the rest of the world how free we were that we failed to safeguard that freedom of which we boasted.

"We commiserate the Englishman because he chooses to live under an hereditary president called a king, while we are amply content to go on living under an elected king called a president. We cannot understand why he, a free citizen of the free-est country on earth, insists on calling himself a subject; but we are reconciled to the fiction of proclaiming ourselves citizens, while each day, more and more, we are becoming subjects--the subjects of sumptuary legislation, the subjects of statutes framed by bigoted or frightened lawgivers, the subjects of arbitrary mandates and of arbitrary decrees, the subjects, the abject, cringing subjects, of the servant classes, the police classes, the labor classes, the capitalistic classes."

Naturally, as a Democrat I have felt these things with enhanced bitterness when the Republicans were in office; nevertheless, I have felt them at other times, too. And, continuing along this line of thought, I have repeatedly said to myself:

"In view of these conditions, let us give 'em the vote--eventually, but not just yet. While still we have control of the machinery of the ballot let us put them on probation, as it were. They claim to be rational creatures; very well, then, make 'em prove it. Let us give 'em the vote just as soon as they have learned the right way in which to get off of a street car."

In this, though, I have changed my mind. I realize now that the demand was impossible, that it was--oh, well, you know what women are!

We have given woman social superiority; rather she has acquired it through having earned it. Shortly she will have been put on a basis of political equality with men in all the states of the Union. Now she thinks she wants economic equality. But she doesn't; she only thinks she does. If she should get it she would refuse to abide by its natural limitations on the one side and its natural expansions for her sphere of economic development on the other. For, temperamentally, God so fashioned her that never can she altogether quit being the clinging vine and become the sturdy oak. She'll insist on having all the prerogatives of the oak, but at the same time she will strive to retain the special considerations accorded to the vine which clings. If I know anything about her dear, wonderful, incomprehensible self, she belongs to the sex which would eat its cake and have it, too. Some men are constructed after this design. But nearly all women are.

Give her equal opportunities with men in business--put her on the same footing and pay to her the same salary that a man holding a similar job is paid. So far so good. But then, as her employer, undertake to hand out to her exactly the same treatment which the man holding a like position expects and accepts. There's where Mr. Boss strikes a snag. The salary she will take--oh, yes--but she arrogates to herself the sweet boon of weeping when things distress her, and, when things harass her, of going off into tantrums of temper which no man in authority, however patient, would tolerate on the part of another man serving under him.

Grant to her equal powers, equal responsibilities, equal favors and a pay envelope on Saturday night containing as much money as her male co-worker receives. That is all very well; but seek, however gently, however tactfully, however diplomatically, to suggest to her that a simpler, more businesslike garb than the garb she favors would be the sane and the sensible thing for business wear in business hours. And then just see what happens.

A working woman who, through the working day, dresses in plain, neat frocks with no jangling bracelets upon her arms, no foolish furbelows at her wrists, no vain adornments about her throat, no exaggerated coiffure, is a delight to the eye and, better still, she fits the setting of her environment. Two of the most competent and dependable human beings I know are both of them women. One is the assistant editor of a weekly magazine. The other is the head of an important department in an important industry. In the evening you would never find a woman better groomed or, if the occasion demand, more ornately rigged-out than either one of these young women will be. But always, while on duty, they wear a correct and proper costume for the work they are doing, and they match the picture. These two, though, are, I think, exceptions to the rule of their sex.

Trained nurses wear the most becoming uniforms, and the most suitable, considering their calling, that were ever devised. To the best of my knowledge and belief there is no record where a marriageable male patient on the road to recovery and in that impressionable mood which accompanies the convalescence of an ordinarily healthy man, failed to fall in love with his nurse. A competent, professional nurse who has the added advantage on her side of being comely--and it is powerfully hard for her to avoid being comely in her spotless blue and starchy white--stands more chances of getting the right sort of man for a husband than any billionaire's daughter alive.

But I sometimes wonder what weird sartorial eccentricities some of them would indulge in did not convention and the standing laws of their profession require of them that they all dress after a given pattern. And if the owners and managers of big city shops once lifted the rule prescribing certain modes for their female working staffs--if they should give their women clerks a free hand in choosing their own wardrobes for store hours--well, you know how women are!

Nevertheless and to the contrary notwithstanding, I will admit while I am on this phase of my topic that there likewise is something to be said in dispraise of my own sex too. In the other--and better half of this literary double sketch-team act, my admired and talented friend, Mrs. Mary Roberts Rinehart, cites chapter and verse to prove the unaccountable vagaries of some men in the matter of dress. There she made but one mistake--a mistake of under-estimation. She mentioned specifically some men; she should have included all men.

The only imaginable reason why any rational he-biped of adult age clings to the habiliments ordained for him by the custom and the tailors of this generation, is because he is used to them. A man can stand anything once he gets used to it because getting used to a thing commonly means that the habitee has quit worrying about it. And yet since the dawn of time when Adam poked fun at Eve's way of wearing her fig-leaf and on down through the centuries until the present day and date it has ever been the custom of men to gibe at the garments worn by women. Take our humorous publications, which I scarcely need point out are edited by men. Hardly could our comic weeklies manage to come out if the jokes about the things which women wear were denied to them as fountain-sources of inspiration. To the vaudeville monologist his jokes about his wife and his mother-in-law and to the comic sketch artist his pictures setting forth the torments of the stock husband trying to button the stock gown of a stock wife up her stock back--these are dependable and inevitable stand-bys.

Women do wear maniacal garments sometimes; that there is no denying. But on the other hand styles for women change with such frequency that no quirk of fashion however foolish and disfiguring ever endures for long enough to work any permanent injury in the health of its temporarily deluded devotees. Nothing I can think of gets old-fashioned with such rapidity as a feminine fashion unless it is an egg.

If this season a woman's skirt is so scantily fashioned that as she hobbles along she has the appearance of being leg-shackled, like the lady called Salammbo, it is as sure as shooting that, come next season, she will have leapt to the other extreme and her draperies will be more than amply voluminous. If this winter her sleeves are like unto sausage casings for tightness, be prepared when spring arrives to see her wearing practically all the sleeves there are. About once in so often she is found wearing a mode which combines beauty with saneness but that often is not very often.

But even when they are at apogee of sartorial ridiculousness I maintain that the garments of women, from the comfort standpoint, anyhow, are not any more foolish than the garments to which the average man is incurably addicted. If women are vassals to fashion men are slaves to convention, and fashion has the merit that it alters overnight, whereas convention is a slow moving thing that stands still a long time before it does move. Convention is the wooden Indian of civilization; but fashion is a merry-go-round.

In the Temperate zone in summertime, Everywoman looks to be cooler than Everyman--and by the same token is cooler. In the winter she wears lighter garments than he would dream of wearing, and yet stays warmer than he does, can stand more exposure without outward evidence of suffering than he can stand, and is less susceptible than he to colds and grips and pneumonias. Compare the thinness of her heaviest outdoor wrap with the thickness of his lightest ulster, or the heft of her so-called winter suit with the weight of the outer garments which he wears to business, and if you are yourself a man you will wonder why she doesn't freeze stiff when the thermometer falls to the twenty-above mark. Observe her in a ballroom that is overheated in the corners and draughty near the windows, as all ballrooms are. Her neck and her throat, her bosom and arms are bare. Her frock is of the filmiest gossamer stuff; her slippers are paper thin, her stockings the sheerest of textures, yet she doesn't sniff and her nose doesn't turn red and the skin upon her exposed shoulders refuses to goose-flesh. She is the marvel of the ages. She is neither too warm nor too cold; she is just right. Consider now her male companion in his gala attire. One minute he is wringing wet with perspiration; that is when he is dancing. The next minute he is visibly congealing. That is because he has stopped to catch his breath.

Why this difference between the sexes? The man is supposed to be the hardier creature of the two, but he can't prove it. Of course there may be something in the theory that when a woman feels herself to be smartly dressed, an exaltation of soul lifts her far above realization of bodily discomfort. But I make so bold as to declare that the real reason why she is comfortable and he is not, lies in the fact that despite all eccentricities of costume in which she sometimes indulges, Everywoman goes about more rationally clad than Everyman does.

For the sake of comparing two horrible examples, let us take a woman esteemed to be over-dressed at all points and angles where she is not under-dressed, and, mentally, let us place alongside her a man who by the standards of his times and his contemporaries is conventionally garbed. To find the woman we want, we probably must travel to New York and seek her out in a smart restaurant at night. Occasionally she is found elsewhere but it is only in New York, that city where so many of the young women are prematurely old and so many of the old women are prematurely young, that she abounds in sufficient profusion to become a common type instead of an infrequent one. This woman is waging that battle against the mounting birthdays which nobody ever yet won. Her hair has been dyed in those rich autumnal tints which are so becoming to a tree in its Indian summer, but so unbecoming to a woman in hers. Richard K. Fox might have designed her jewelry; she glistens with diamonds until she makes you think of the ice coming out of the Hudson River in the early spring. But about her complexion there is no suggestion of a March thaw. For it is a climate-proof shellac. Her eyebrows are the self-made kind, and her lips were done by hand. Her skirt is too short for looks and too tight for comfort; she is tightly prisoned at the waistline and not sufficiently confined in the bust. There is nothing natural or rational anywhere about her. She is as artificial as a tin minnow and she glitters like one.

Next your attention is invited to the male of the species. He is assumed to be dressed in accordance with the dictates of good taste and with due regard for all the ordinary proprieties. But is he? Before deciding whether he is or isn't, let us look him over, starting from the feet and working upward. A matter of inches above his insteps brings us to the bottom of his trouser-legs. Now these trouser-legs of his are morally certain to be too long, in which event they billow down over his feet in slovenly and ungraceful folds, or they are too short, in which event there is an awkward, ugly cross-line just above his ankles. If he is a thin man, his dress waistcoat bulges away from his breastbone so the passerby can easily discover what brand of suspenders he fancies; but if he be stoutish, the waistcoat has a little way of hitching along up his mid-riff inch by inch until finally it has accordion-pleated itself in overlapping folds thwartwise of his tummy, coyly exposing an inch or so of clandestine shirt-front.

It requires great will-power on the part of the owner and constant watchfulness as well to keep a fat man's dress waistcoat from behaving like a railroad folder. His dinner coat or his tail coat, if he wears a tail coat, is invariably too tight in the sleeves; nine times out of ten it binds across the back between the shoulders, and bulges out in a pouch effect at the collar. His shirt front, if hard-boiled, is as cold and clammy as a morgue slab when first he puts it on; but as hot and sticky as a priming of fresh glue after he has worn it for half an hour in an overheated room--and all public rooms in America are overheated. Should it be of the pleated or medium well-done variety, no power on earth can keep it from appearing rumply and untidy; that is, no power can if the wearer be a normal man. I am not speaking of professional he-beauties or models for the illustrations of haberdashers' advertisements in the magazines. His collar, which is a torturer's device of stiff linen and yielding starch, is not a comparatively modern product as some have imagined. It really dates back to the Spanish Inquisition where it enjoyed a great vogue. Faring abroad, he encloses his head, let us say in a derby hat. Some people think the homeliest thing ever devised by man is Grant's Tomb. Others favor the St. Louis Union Depot. But I am pledged to the derby hat. And the high or two-quart hat runs second.

This being the case for and against the parties concerned, I submit to the reader's impartial judgment the following question for a decision: Taking everything into consideration, which of these two really deserves the booby prize for unbecoming apparel--the woman who plainly is dressed in bad form or the man who is supposed to be dressed in good form? But this I will say for him as being in his favor. He has sense enough to wear plenty of pockets. And in his most infatuated moments he never wears nether garments so tight that he can't step in 'em. Can I say as much for woman? I cannot.

A few pages back I set up the claim that woman, considered as a sex and not as an exceptional type, cannot divorce the social relation from the economic. I think of an illustration to prove my point: In business two men may be closely associated. They may be room-mates besides; chums, perhaps, at the same club; may borrow money from each other and wear each other's clothes; and yet, so far as any purely confidential relation touching on the private sides of their lives is concerned, may remain as far apart as the poles.

It is hard to imagine two women, similarly placed, behaving after the same common-sense standards. Each insists upon making a confidante of her partner. Their intimacy becomes a thing complicated with extraneous issues, with jointly shared secrets, with disclosures as to personal likes and dislikes, which should have no part in it if there is to be continued harmony, free from heart-burnings or lacerated feelings, or fancied slights or blighted affections. Sooner or later, too, the personality of the stronger nature begins to overshadow the personality of the weaker. Almost inevitably there is a falling-out.

I do not share the somewhat common opinion that in their friendships women are less constant than men are. But the trouble with them is that they put a heavier burden upon friendship than so delicate, so sensitive a sentiment as real friendship is was ever meant to bear. Something has to give way under the strain. And something does.

To be sure there is an underlying cause in extenuation for this temperamental shortcoming which in justice to the ostensibly weaker sex should be set forth here. Even though I am taking on the rôle of Devil's Advocate in the struggle to keep woman from canonizing herself by main force I want to be as fair as I can, always reserving the privilege where things are about even, of giving my own side a shade the better of it. The main tap-root reason why women confide over-much and too much in other women is because leading more circumscribed lives than men commonly lead they are driven back upon themselves and into themselves and their sisters for interests and for conversational material.

Taking them by and large they have less with which to concern themselves than their husbands and their brothers, their fathers and their sons have. Therefore they concern themselves the more with what is available, which, at the same time, oftener than not, means some other woman's private affairs.

A woman, becoming thoroughly imbued with an idea, becomes, ninety-nine times out of a hundred, a creature of one idea. Everything else on earth is subordinated to the thing--cabal, reform, propaganda, crusade, movement or what not--in which she is interested. Now the average man may be very sincerely and very enthusiastically devoted to a cause; but it does not necessarily follow that it will obsess him through every waking hour. But the ladies, God bless 'em--and curb 'em--are not built that way. A woman wedded to a cause is divorced from all else. She resents the bare thought that in the press of matters and the clash of worlds, mankind should for one moment turn aside from her pet cause to concern itself with newer issues and wider motives. From a devotee she soon is transformed into a habitee. From being an earnest advocate she advances--or retrogrades--to the status of a plain bore. To be a common nuisance is bad enough; to be a common scold is worse, and presently she turns scold and goes about railing shrilly at a world that criminally persists in thinking of other topics than the one which lies closest to her heart and loosest on her tongue.

Than a woman who is a scold there is but one more exasperating shape of a woman and that is the woman who, not content with being the most contradictory, the most paradoxical, the most adorable of the Almighty's creations--to wit, a womanly woman--tries, among men, to be a good fellow, so-called.

But that which is ordinarily a fault may, on occasion of extraordinary stress, become the most transcendent and the most admirable of virtues. I think of this last war and of the share our women and the women of other lands have played in it. No one caviled nor complained at the one-ideaness of womankind while the world was in a welter of woe and slaughter. Of all that they had, worth having, our women gave and gave and gave and gave. They gave their sons and their brothers, their husbands and their fathers, to their country; they gave of their time and of their energies and of their talent; they gave of their wonderful mercy and their wonderful patience, and their yet more wonderful courage; they gave of the work of their hands and the salt of their souls and the very blood of their hearts. For every suspected woman slacker there were ten known men slackers--yea, ten times ten and ten to carry.

Each day, during that war, the story of Mary Magdalene redeemed was somewhere lived over again. Every great crisis in the war-torn lands produced its Joan of Arc, its Florence Nightingale, its Clara Barton. To the women fell the tasks which for the most part brought no public recognition, no published acknowledgments of gratitude. For them, instead of the palms of victory and the sheaves of glory, there were the crosses of sacrifice, the thorny diadems of suffering. We cannot conceive of men, thus circumstanced, going so far and doing so much. But the women--

Oh, well, you know how women are!

"ISN'T THAT JUST LIKE A MAN!"

BY MARY ROBERTS RINEHART

Author of "Dangerous Days," "The Amazing Interlude," "K," etc.

NEW YORK GEORGE H. DORAN COMPANY

"ISN'T THAT JUST LIKE A MAN!"

I understand that Mr. Irvin Cobb is going to write a sister article to this, and naturally he will be as funny as only he can be. It is always allowable, too, to be humorous about women. They don't mind, because they are accustomed to it.

But I simply dare not risk my popularity by being funny about men. Why, bless their hearts (Irvin will probably say of his subject, "bless their little hearts." Odd, isn't it, how men always have big hearts and women little ones? But we are good packers. We put a lot in 'em) I could be terribly funny, if only women were going to read this. They'd understand. They know all about men. They'd go up-stairs and put on a negligee and get six baby pillows and dab a little cold cream around their eyes and then lie down on the couch and read, and they would all think I must have known their men-folks somewhere.

But the men would read it and cancel the order for my next book, and say I must be a spinster, living a sort of in-bred existence. Why, I know at least a hundred good stories about one man alone, and if I published them he would either grow suspicious and wonder who the man is, or, get sulky and resent bitterly being laughed at! Which is exactly like a man. Just little things, too, like always insisting he was extremely calm at his wedding, when the entire church saw him step off a platform and drop seven feet into tropical foliage.

You see, women quite frequently have less wit than men, but they don't take themselves quite so seriously; they view themselves with a certain somewhat ironical humor. Men love a joke--on the other fellow. But your really humorous woman loves a joke on herself. That's because women are less conventional, of course. I can still remember the face of the horrified gentleman I met one day on the street after luncheon, who had unconsciously tucked the corner of his luncheon napkin into his watch pocket along with his watch, and his burning shame when I observed that his new fashion was probably convenient but certainly novel.

And I contrast it with the woman, prominent in the theatrical world, who had been doing a little dusting--yes, they do, but it is never published--before coming to lunch with me. She walked into one of the largest of the New York hotels, hatted, veiled and sable-ed, and wearing tied around her waist a large blue-and-white checked gingham apron.

Now I opine (I have stolen that word from Irvin) that under those circumstances, or something approximating them, such as pajama trousers, or the neglect to conceal that portion of a shirt not intended for the public eye, almost any man of my acquaintance would have made a wild bolt for the nearest bar, hissing like a teakettle. Note: This was written when the word bar did not mean to forbid or to prohibit. The gingham-apron lady merely stood up smilingly, took it off and gave it to the waiter, who being a man returned it later wrapped to look as much like a club sandwich as possible.

Oh, they're conventional, these men, right enough! Now and then one of them gathers a certain amount of courage and goes without a hat to save his hair, or wears sandals to keep his feet cool, and he is immediately dismissed as mad. I know one very young gentleman who nearly broke up a juvenile dance by borrowing his mother's pink silk stockings for socks and wearing her best pink ribbon as a tie.

How many hours do you suppose were wasted by the new army practicing salutes in front of a mirror? A good many right arms to-day, back in "civies," have a stuttering fit whenever they approach a uniform. And I know a number of conventional gentlemen who are suffering hours of torment because they can't remember, out of uniform, to take off their hats to the women they meet. War is certainly perdition, isn't it? And numbers of times during the late unpleasantness I have seen new officers standing outside a general's door, trying to remember the rule for addressing a superior, and cap or no cap while not wearing side arms.

You know how a woman would do it. She would give a tilt to her hat and a pull here and there, and then she would walk in and say:

"I know it's perfectly horrible, but I simply can't remember the etiquette of this sort of thing. Please do tell me, General."

And the general, who has only eleven hundred things to do before eating a bite of lunch on the top of his desk, will get up and gravely instruct her. Which is exactly like a man, of course.

Men overdo etiquette sometimes, because of a conventional fear of slipping up somewhere. There was a nice Red Cross major in France who had had no instruction in military matters, and had no arrogance whatever. So he used to salute all the privates and the M. P.'s before they had a chance. He was usually asking the road to somewhere or other, and they would stand staring after him thoughtfully until he was quite out of sight.

And as a corollary to this conventionality, how wretched men are when they are placed in false positions! Nobody likes it, of course, but a woman can generally get out of it. Men think straighter than women, but not so fast. I dined one night on shipboard with the captain of the transport on which I came back from France, and there was an army chaplain at the table. So, as chaplains frequently say grace before meat, I put a hand on the knee of a young male member of my family beside me and kept it there, ready for a squeeze to admonish silence. But the chaplain did not say grace, and the man on my right suddenly turned out to be a perfectly strange general in a state of helpless uneasiness. I have a suspicion that not even the absolute impeccability of my subsequent conduct convinced him that I was not a designing woman.

But, although we are discussing men, as all women know, there are really no men at all. There are grown-up boys, and middle-aged boys, and elderly boys, and even sometimes very old boys. But the essential difference is simply exterior. Your man is always a boy. He grows tidier, and he gathers up a mass of heterogeneous information, and in the strangest possible fashion as the years go on, boards have to be put into the dining-room table, and the shoe bill becomes something terrible, and during some of his peregrinations he feels rather like a comet with a tail. The dentist's bills and where to go for the summer and do-you-think-the-nurse-is-as-careful-as-she-should-be-with-baby's-bottles make him put on a sort of surface maturity. But it never fools his womankind. Deep down he still believes in Santa Claus, and would like to get up at dawn on the Fourth of July and throw a firecracker through the cook's window.

That is the reason women are natural monogamists. They know they have to be one-man women, because the one man is so always a boy, and has to have so much mothering and looking after. He has to be watched for fear his hair gets too long, and sent to the tailor's now and then for clothes. And if someone didn't turn his old pajamas into scrub rags and silver cloths, he would go on wearing their ragged skeletons long after the flesh had departed hence. (What comforting rags Irvin Cobb's pajamas must make!)

And then of course now and then he must be separated forcibly from his old suits and shoes. The best method, as every woman knows, is to give them to someone who is going on a long, long journey, else he will follow and bring them back in triumph. This fondness for what is old is a strange thing in men. It does not apply to other things--save cheese and easy chairs and some kinds of game and drinkables. In the case of caps, boots, and trousers it is akin to mania. It sometimes applies to dress waistcoats and evening ties, but has one of its greatest exacerbations (beat that word, Irvin) in the matter of dressing gowns. If by any chance a cigarette has burned a hole in the dressing gown, it takes on the additional interest of survival, and is always hung, hole out, where company can see it.

Full many a gentleman, returning from the wars, has found that his heart's treasures have gone to rummage sales, and--you know the story of the man who bought his dress suit back for thirty-five cents.

I am personally acquainted with a man who owns a number of pairs of bedroom slippers, nice leather ones, velvet ones, felt ones. They sit in a long row in his closet, and sit and sit. And when that man prepares for his final cigarette at night--and to drop asleep and burn another hole in his dressing gown, or in the chintz chair cover, or the carpet, as Providence may will it--he wears on his feet a pair of red knitted bedroom slippers with cords that tie around the top and dangle and trip him up. Long years ago they stretched, and they have been stretching ever since, until now each one resembles an afghan.

Will he give them up? He will not.

There is something feline about a man's love for old, familiar things. I know that it is a popular misconception to compare women with cats and men with dogs. But the analogy is clearly the other way.

Just run over the cat's predominant characteristic and check them off: The cat is a night wanderer. The cat loves familiar places, and the hearthside. (And, oddly enough, the cat's love of the hearthside doesn't interfere with his night wanderings!) The cat can hide under the suavest exterior in the world principles that would make a kitten blush if it had any place for a blush. The cat is greedy as to helpless things. And heavens, how the cat likes to be petted and generally approved! It likes love, but not all the time. And it likes to choose the people it consorts with. It is a predatory creature, also, and likes to be neat and tidy, while it sticks to its old trousers with a love that passeth understanding--there, I've slipped up, but you know what I mean.

Now women are like dogs, really. They love like dogs, a little insistently. And they like to fetch and carry, and come back wistfully after hard words, and learn rather easily to carry a basket. And after three years or so of marriage they learn to enjoy the bones of conversation and sometimes even to go to the mat with them. (Oh, Irvin, I know that's dreadful!) Really, the only resemblance between men and dogs is that they both rather run to feet in early life.

This fondness for old clothes and old chairs and familiar places is something women find hard to understand. Yet it is simple enough. It is compounded of comfort and loyalty.

Men are curiously loyal. They are loyal to ancient hats and disreputable old friends and to some women. But they are always loyal to each other.

This, I maintain, is the sole reason for alluding to them as the stronger and superior sex. They are stronger. They are superior. They are as strong as a trades union, only more so. They stand together against the rest of the world. Women do not. They have no impulse toward solidarity. They fight a sort of guerilla warfare, each sniping from behind her own tree. They are the greatest example of the weakness of unorganized force in the world.

But this male trades union is not due to affection. It is two-fold. It is a survival from the days when men united for defense. Women didn't unite. They didn't need to, and they couldn't have, anyhow. When the cave man went away to fight or to do the family marketing, he used to roll a large bowlder against the entrance to his stone mansion, and thus discouraged afternoon callers of the feminine sex who would otherwise have dropped in for a cup of tea. Then he took away the rope ladder and cut off the telephone, and went away with a heart at peace to join the other males.

They would do it now, if they could.

But the real reason for their sex solidarity is their terrible alikeness. They understand each other. Knowing their own weaknesses, they know the other fellow's. So they stand by each other, sometimes out of sympathy, and occasionally out of fear. You see, it is not only a trades union, it is a mutual benefit society. Its only constitution is the male Golden Rule--"You stick by me and I'll stick by you." "We men must stick together."

I'll confess that with a good many women it is, "You stick me and I'll stick you."

But that solidarity, primarily offensive and defensive, has also an element in it that women seldom understand, and almost always resent. Not very many years ago a play ran in New York without a woman in the cast or connected with the story. There is one running very successfully now in Paris. Both were written by men, naturally. Women cannot conceive of the drama of life without women in it. But men can.

The plain truth is that normal women need men all the time, but that normal men need women only a part of the time. They like to have them to go back to, but they do not need them in sight, or even within telephone call. There are some hours of every day when you could repeat a man's wife's name to him through a megaphone, and he would have to come a long ways back, from golf or pool or the ticker or the stock news, to remember who she is.

When a man gets up a golf foursome he wants four men. When a woman does it, she wants three.

It is this ability to be happy without her that a woman never understands. Her lack of understanding of it causes a good bit of unhappiness, too. Men are gregarious; they like to be together. But women gauge them by their own needs, and form dark surmises about these harmless meetings, which are as innocuous and often as interesting as the purely companionable huddlings of sheep in pasture.

Women play bridge together to fill in the time until the five-thirty is due. Men play bridge because they like to beat the other fellow.

Mind you, I am not saying there are not strong and fine affections among women. If it comes to that, there is often deeper devotion, perhaps, than among men. But I am saying that women do not care for women as a sex, as men care for men. Men will die to save other men. Women will sacrifice themselves ruthlessly for children, but not for other women. Queer, isn't it?

Yet not so queer. Women want marriage and a home. They should. And there are more women than men. Even before the war there was, in Europe and America, an extra sixth woman for every five men, and the sixth woman brings competition. She bulls the market, and makes feminine sex solidarity impossible. And, of course, added to that is the woman who requires three or four men to make her happy, one to marry and support her, and one to take her to the theater and to luncheon at Delmonico's, and generally fetch and carry for her, and one to remember her as she was at nineteen and remain a bachelor and have a selfish, delightful life, while blaming her. This makes masculine stock still higher, and as there are always buyers on a rising market, competition among women--purely unconscious competition--flourishes.

So men hang together, and women don't. And men are the stronger sex because they are fewer!

Obviously the cure is the elimination of that sixth woman, preferably by euthanasia. (Look this up, Irvin. It's a good one.) That sixth woman ought to go. She has made men sought and not seekers. She ruins dinner parties and is the vampire of the moving pictures. And after living a respectable life for years she either goes on living a respectable life, and stays with her sister's children while the family goes on a motor tour, or takes to serving high-balls instead of afternoon tea, while wearing a teagown of some passionate shade.

It is just possible that suffrage will bring women together. It is just possible that male opposition has in it this subconscious fear, that their superiority is thus threatened. They don't really want equality, you know. They love to patronize us a bit, bless them; and to tell us to run along and not bother our little heads about things that don't concern us. And, of course, politics has been their own private maneuvering ground, and--I have made it clear, I think, that they don't always want us--here we are, about to drill on it ourselves, perhaps drilling a mite better than they do in some formations, and standing right on their own field and telling them the mistakes they've made, and not to take themselves too hard and that the whole game is a lot easier than they have always pretended it was.

They don't like it, really, a lot of them. Their solidarity is threatened. Their superiority, and another sanctuary, as closed to women as a monastery, or a club, is invaded. No place to go but home.

Yet I have a sneaking sympathy for them. They were so terribly happy running things, and fighting wars, and coming back at night to throw their conversational bones around the table. It is rather awful to think of them coming home now and having some little woman say:

"Certainly we are not going to the movies. Don't you know there is a ward caucus to-night?"

There is a curious situation in the economic world, too. Business has been the man's field ever since Cain and Abel went into the stock and farming combine, with one of them raising grain for the other's cows, and taking beef in exchange. And the novelty is gone. But there's a truism here: Men play harder than they work; women work harder than they play.

Women in business bring to it the freshness of novelty, and work at their maximum as a sex. Men, being always boys, work *under* their maximum. (Loud screams here. But think it over! How about shaking dice at the club after lunch, and wandering back to the office at three P M to sign the mail? How about golf? I'll wager I work more hours a day than you, Irvin!)

The plain truth is that if more men put their whole hearts into business during business hours, there would be no question of competition. As I have said, they think straighter than women, although more slowly. They have more physical strength. They don't have sick headaches--unless they deserve them. But they are vaguely resentful when some little woman, who has washed the children and sent them off to school and straightened her house and set out a cold lunch, comes into the office at nine o'clock and works in circles all around them.

But there is another angle to this "woman in the business world" idea that puzzles women. Not long ago a clever woman whose husband does not resent her working, since his home and children are well looked after, said to me:

"I've always been interested in what he had to say of his day at the office, but he doesn't seem to care at all about *my* day. He seems so awfully self-engrossed."

The truth probably is that they are both self-engrossed, but women can dissemble and men cannot. It is another proof of their invincible boyishness, this total inability to pretend interest. Even the averagest man is no hypocrite. He tries it sometimes, and fails pitifully. The successful male dissembler is generally a crook. But the most honest woman in the world is often driven to pretense, although she may call it *savoir faire*. She pretends, because pretense is the oil that lubricates society. Have you ever seen a man when some neighbors who are unpopular drop in for an evening call? After they are gone, his wife says:

"I do wish you wouldn't bite the Andersons when they come in, Joe!"

"Bite them! I was civil, wasn't I?"

"Well, you can call it that."

He is ready to examine the window locks, but he turns and surveys her, and he is honestly puzzled.

"What I can't make out," he says, "is how you can fall all over yourself to those people, when you know you detest them. Thank heavens, I'm no hypocrite."

Then he locks the windows and stalks up-stairs, and the hypocrite of the family smiles a little to herself. Because she knows that without her there would be no society and no neighborhood calls, and that honesty can be a vice, and hypocrisy a virtue.

I know a vestryman of a church who sometimes plays bridge on Saturday nights for money. What he loses doesn't matter, but what he wins his wife is supposed to put on the plate the next morning. One Saturday night he gave her a large bill, and the next morning she placed a neatly folded green-back on the collection plate as he held it out to her. He stood in the aisle and eyed the bill with suspicion. Then he deliberately unfolded it, and held out the plate to her again.

"Come over, Mazie," he said.

And Mazie came over with the balance.

You know what a woman would have done. She would have marked the bill with her eye, and later on while waiting at the rear for the chair offertory to end, she would have investigated. Then on the way home she would have said:

"I had a good notion to stand right there, Charlie Smith, and show you up. I wish I had." But the point is that she wouldn't have.

There is no moral whatever to this brief tale.

But perhaps it is in love that men and women differ most vitally. Now Nature, being extremely wise, gives the man in love the wisdom of the serpent and the wile of the dove (which is a most alluring bird in its love-making). A man in love brings to it all his intelligence. And men like being in love.

Being in love is not so happy for a woman. She becomes emotional and difficult, is either on the heights or in the depths. And the reason for this is simple; love is a complex to a woman. She has to contend with natural and acquired inhibitions. She both desires love and fears it.

The primitive woman ran away from her lover, but like Lot's wife, she looked back. I am inclined to think, however, that primitive woman looked back rather harder than she ran. Be that as it may, women to-day both desire love and fear it.

If men fear it, they successfully hide their cowardice.

It is in their methods of making love that men cease to be alike. Up to that point they are very similar; they all think that, having purchased an automobile, they must vindicate their judgment by insisting upon its virtues, and a great many of them will spend as much money fixing over last year's car as would almost buy a new one; they always think they drive carefully, but that the fellow in the other car is either a road hog or a lunatic who shouldn't have a license; they are mostly rather moody before breakfast, although there is an obnoxious type that sings in the cold shower; they are all rather given to the practice of bringing gifts to their wives when they have done something they shouldn't; and they all have a tendency to excuse their occasional delinquencies by the argument that they never made anybody unhappy, and their weaknesses by the fact that God made them men.

But it is in love that they are at their best, from the point of view of the one woman most interested. And it is in their love methods that they show the greatest variations from type. Certain things of course they all do, buy new neckties, write letters which they read years later with amazement and consternation; keep a photograph in a drawer of the desk at the office, where the stenographer finds it and says to the office boy: "Can you beat that? And not even pretty!" carry boxes of candy around, hoping they look like cigars; and lie awake nights wondering what she can see in him, and wondering if she is awake too.

They are very dear and very humble and sheepish and self-conscious when they are in love, curious mixtures of determination and vacillation; about eighty per cent, however, being determination. But they lose for once their sex solidarity, and play the game every man for himself. Roughly speaking (although who can speak roughly of them then? Or at any time?) they divide into three types of lovers. There are men who are all three, at different times of course. But these three classes of lovers have one thing in common. They want to do their own hunting. It gives them a sense of power to think they have won out by sheer strength and will.

The truth about this is that no man ever won a woman who was actually difficult to get, and found it worth the effort afterwards. What real man ever liked kissing a girl who didn't want to be kissed? Love has got to be mutual. Your lover is frequently more interested in being loved than in loving. And the trump cards are always the woman's. These grown-up boys of ours are shy and self-depreciatory in love, and they run like deer when they think they are not wanted. So the woman has to play a double game, and gets blamed for guile when it is only wisdom. Her instinct is to run, partly because she is afraid of love and partly because she has to appear to be pursued. But she has to limp a bit, and sit down and look back rather wistfully, and in the end of course she goes lame entirely and is overtaken.

This is the same instinct which makes the pheasant hen feign a broken wing.

There is a wonderful type of woman, however, who goes as straight to the man she loves as a homing pigeon to its loft.

Taking, then, the three classes of men in the throes of the disease of love, we have the following symptoms, diagnosis and prognosis.

First. The average lover. Temperature remains normal, with slight rise in the evenings. Continues to attend to business. Feeling of uneasiness if called by endearing names over office 'phone. Regular diet, but smokes rather too much. Anxiety strongly marked as to how his income will cover a house and garage in the country, adding the cost of his commutation ticket, and shows tendency to look rather wistfully into toy shop-windows before Christmas.

Diagnosis: Normal love.

Prognosis: Probably permanent condition.[1]

Second. The fearful lover. Temperature inclined to be sub-normal at times. Physical type, a hulking brute of a man, liking small women, only he feels coarse and rather gross when with them. He is the physical type generally attributed to the cave man, but this is an error. (See cave man, later.) His timidity is not physical but mental, and is referable by the Freud theory to his early youth, when he was taught that big, overgrown boys did not tease kittens, but put them in their pockets and carried them home. Has the kitten obsession still. Is six months getting up enough courage to squeeze a five-and-a-half hand, and then crushes it to death. Reads poetry, and is very early for all appointments. Appetite small. Does not sleep. In small communities shows occasional semi-paralysis on the curb after Sunday evening service, and lets a fellow half his size see her home. (See cave man, later.) Is always in love, but not with the same woman. Is easily hurt, and walks it off on Sunday afternoons. Telephones with gentle persistence, and prefers the movies to the theater because they are dark. This type sometimes loses its gentleness after marriage, and always has an ideal woman in mind. Some one who walks like Pauline Frederick and smiles like Mary Pickford.[2]

Diagnosis: Normal love, with idealistic complications.

Prognosis: Condition less permanent than in case A, as less essentially monogamous. Should be careful not to carry the search for the ideal to excess.

Third. The cave man. Temperature normally high, with dangerous rises. Physique rather under-sized, with prominent Adam's apple. Is attracted by large women, whom he dominates. Is assured, violent and jealous. Appetite fastidious. Takes sleeping powders during course of disease and uses telephone frequently to find out if the object of his affections is lunching with another man. Is extremely possessive as to women, and has had in early years a strong desire to take the other fellow's girl away from him. Is pugnacious and intelligent, but has moments of great tenderness and charm. Shows his worst side to the neighbors and breathes freely after nine o'clock P.M., when no one has come to call.[3]

Diagnosis: Normal love, with jealousy.

Prognosis: A large family of daughters.

A great many women believe that they can change men by marrying them. This is a mistake. Women make it because they themselves are pliable, but the male is firmly fixed at the age of six years, and remains fundamentally the same thereafter. The only way to make a husband over according to one's ideas then would be to adopt him at an early age, say four. But who really wants to change them? Where would be the interest in marriage? To tell the truth, we like their weaknesses. It gives women that entirely private conviction they have that John would make an utter mess of things if they were not around.

Men know better how to live than women. The average man gets more out of life than the average woman. He compounds his days, if he be a healthy, normal individual, of work and play, and his play generally takes the form of fresh air and exercise. He has, frequently, more real charity than his womankind, and by charity I mean an understanding of human weakness and a tolerance of frailty. He may dislike his neighbors heartily, and snub them in prosperity, but in trouble he is quick with practical assistance. And although often tactless, for tact and extreme honesty are incompatible, he is usually kind. There is often a selfish purpose behind his altruism, his broad charitable organizations. But to individual cases of distress he is generous, unselfish, and sacrificing.

In politics he is individually honest, as a rule, but collectively corrupt. And this strange and disheartening fact is due to lethargy. He is politically indolent, so he allows the few to rule, and this few is too frequently in political life for what it can get and not what it can give. Sins of omission may be grave sins.

Yet he is individually honest in politics, and in most things, and that, partly at least, is because, pretty much overlaid with worldliness, he has a deep religious conviction. But he has a terrible fear of letting anyone know he has it. Indeed, he is shamefaced about all his emotions. He would sooner wear two odd shoes than weep at a funeral.

Really, this article could run on forever. There's that particularly manlike attitude of accusing women of slavishly following the fashions! Funny, isn't it, when you think about it? Do you think a man would wear a striped tie with a morning coat when his haberdasher says others are wearing plain gray? Or a straw hat before the fifteenth of May? Have you ever watched the mental struggle between a dinner suit and evening clothes? Do you suppose that women, realizing that the costume they wore was the ugliest ever devised, would continue wearing it because everyone else did? And then look at men's trousers and derby hats!

It is men who are the slaves, double chained, of fashion. The only comfortable innovation in men's clothes made in a century was when some brave spirit originated the shirtwaist man. Women saw its comfort, adopted and retained the shirtwaist. But the leaders of male fashion dictated that comfort was bad form, and on went all the coats again. Irvin Cobb is undoubtedly going to say that it is just like a woman to wear no flannels in winter, and silk hose, and generally go about half clad. But men are as over-dressed in summer as women are under-dressed in winter.

But in spite of this slavish following of fashion, men are really more rational than women. They have the same mental processes. For that reason they understand each other. Like the village fool who found the lost horse by thinking where he would go if he were a horse, a man knows what another man will do by fancying himself in the same circumstances. And women are called designing because they have fathomed this fundamental simplicity of the male! A woman's emotions and her sensations and her thoughts are all complexes. She doesn't know herself what she is going to do, and is frequently more astounded than anyone else at what she does do. It's a lot harder being a woman than a man.

So--women know men better than men know women, and are rather like the little boy's definition of a friend: "A friend is a feller who knows all about you, and likes you anyhow."

We do like them, dreadfully. Sometimes women have sighed and wondered what the house would be like without overcoats thrown about in the hall, and every closet full of beloved old ragged clothes and shoes, and cigar ashes over things, and wild cries for the ancient hat they gave the gardener last week to weed in. But quite recently the women of this country and a lot of other countries have found out what even temporary absence means. A house without a man in it is as nice and tidy and peaceful and attractive and cheerful as a grave in a cemetery. It is as pleasant as Mark Twain's celebrated combination of rheumatism and St. Vitus dance, and as empty as a penny-in-the-slot chocolate machine in a railway station.

Not so very long ago there was a drawing in one of the magazines. It showed a row of faces, men with hooked noses, with cauliflower ears, with dish-faces, and flat faces, with smallpox scars, with hare lips. And underneath it said: "Never mind, every one of them is somebody's darling."

Women don't really care how their men look. But they want to look up to them--which is a reason I haven't given before for their sex superiority. It is really forced on them! And they want them kind and even a bit patronizing. Also they want them *well*, because a sick man can come the closest thing in the world to biting the hand that feeds him. And loyal, of course, and not too tidy--and to be hungry at meals. And not to be too bitter about going out in the evenings.

And the one thing they do not want is to have their men know how well they understand them. It is one of their pet little-boy conceits, this being misunderstood. It has survived from the time of that early punishment when each and every one of them contemplated running off and going to sea. Most of them still contemplate that running off. They visualize great spaces, and freedom, and tropic isles, and--well, you know. "Where there ain't no Ten Commandments and a man can raise a thirst." (You know, Irvin!)

Yes, they contemplate it every now and then, and then they go home, and put on a fresh collar for dinner, and examine the vegetable garden, and take the children out in the machine for a few minutes' fresh air, and have a pillow fight in the nursery, and--forget the other thing.

Which is exactly like a man.

[1] Will probably forget small attentions to his wife after marriage.

[2] Will always remember small attentions to his wife after marriage, especially when conscience troubles him.

[3] Receives constant attention from his family after marriage.